FAITHFUL FEET

Written by Laura Sassi Illustrated by Emanuela Di Donna

Inspired by Isaiah 52:7

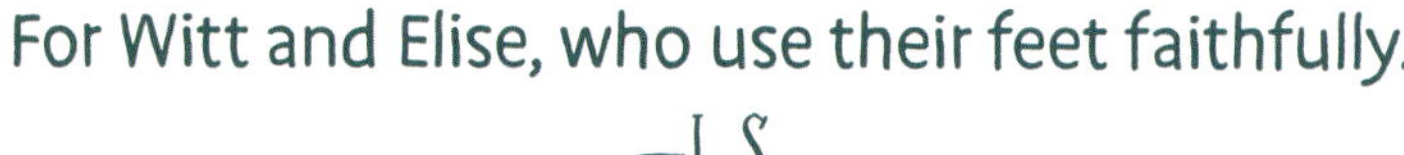

For Witt and Elise, who use their feet faithfully.
—L.S.

To Mom and Dad. And to Antonio, Emilio, Simona, Ale, and all my family. Thank you.
—E.D.D.

ISBN: 978-1-5460-0763-0

WorthyKids
Hachette Book Group
1290 Avenue of the Americas
New York, NY 10104

Library of Congress Cataloging-in-Publication Data
Names: Sassi, Laura, author. | Di Donna, Emanuela, illustrator.
Title: Faithful Feet / by Laura Sassi ; illustrated by Emanuela Di Donna.
Description: New York, NY : WorthyKids, 2025. | Audience: Ages 4 to 7. | Audience: Grades K–1.
Summary: "This whimsical rhyming picture book highlights how God's people have used their feet, from Bible times to modern day, to bring God's love to others"—Provided by publisher.
Identifiers: LCCN 2024016799 | ISBN 9781546007630 (hardcover)
Subjects: CYAC: Stories in rhyme. | Faith. | Foot. | Christian Life—Fiction. | LCGFT: Stories in rhyme. | Picture books. | Christian fiction.
Classification: LCC PZ8.3.S237 Fa 2025 | DDC [E]—dc23
LC record available at https://lccn.loc.gov/2024016799

Designed by John Trent

Printed and bound in Dongguan, China • APS • 10 9 8 7 6 5 4 3 2 1

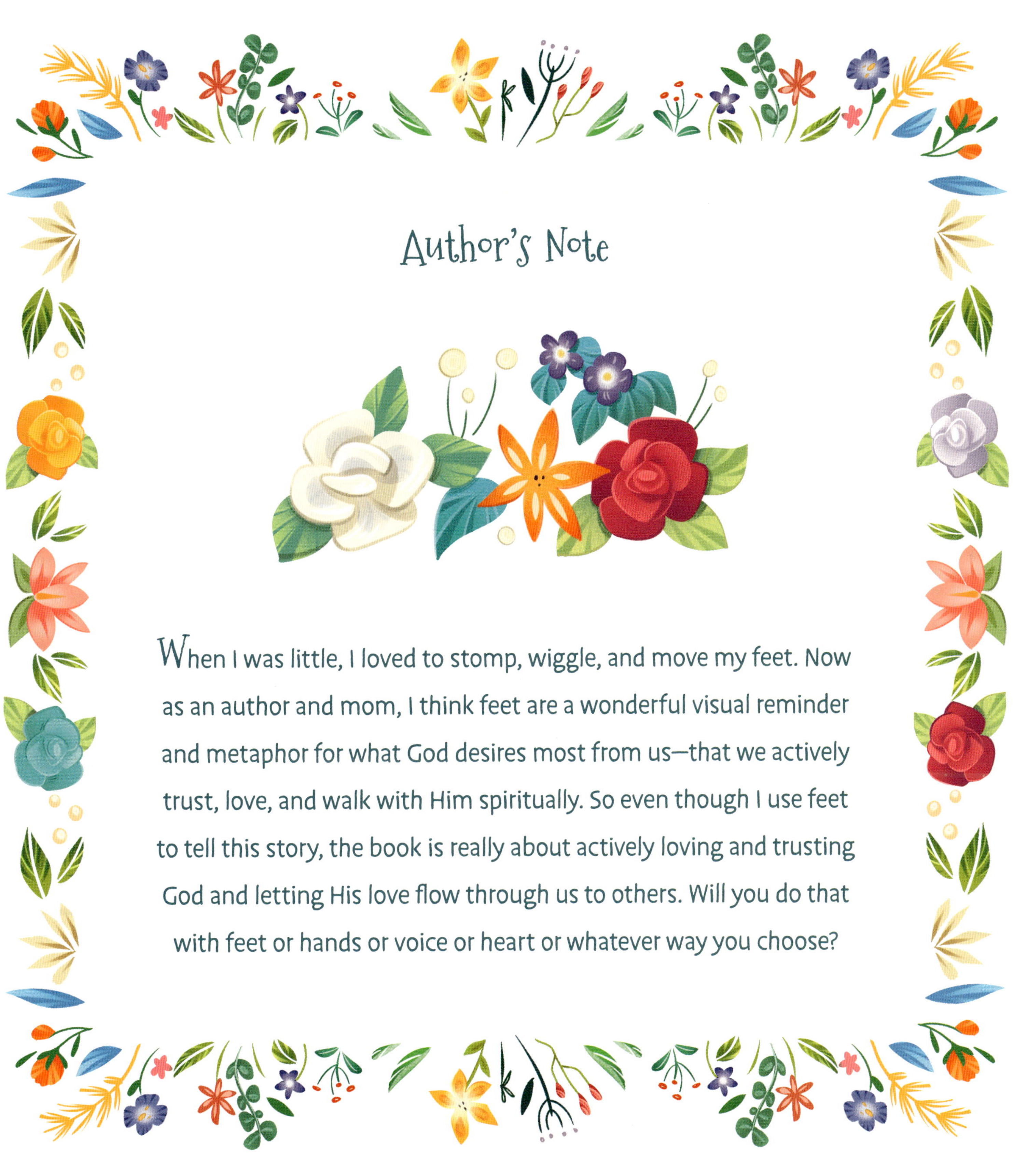

Author's Note

When I was little, I loved to stomp, wiggle, and move my feet. Now as an author and mom, I think feet are a wonderful visual reminder and metaphor for what God desires most from us—that we actively trust, love, and walk with Him spiritually. So even though I use feet to tell this story, the book is really about actively loving and trusting God and letting His love flow through us to others. Will you do that with feet or hands or voice or heart or whatever way you choose?

Feet are funny! Don't you think?
They poke. They plod. They plink. They stink!

Some are lean and some are chubby.
Some are clean and some are grubby.

But here is something super neat:

God loves it
when you use your feet.
And in the Bible, pair by pair,
you can find feet everywhere!

Noah's hairy feet were good
for making trips to gather wood
to build the ark that through the storm
would keep God's creatures safe and warm.

Trusting in God's faithful care,
even in the lion's lair,
Daniel showed by **standing strong**
that God was with him all along.

And when Goliath stood so tall,
scaring soldiers big and small,
David stepped in faith alone
and knocked him down with just one stone!

Now look at Mary's dusty feet,
as she traveled in the heat

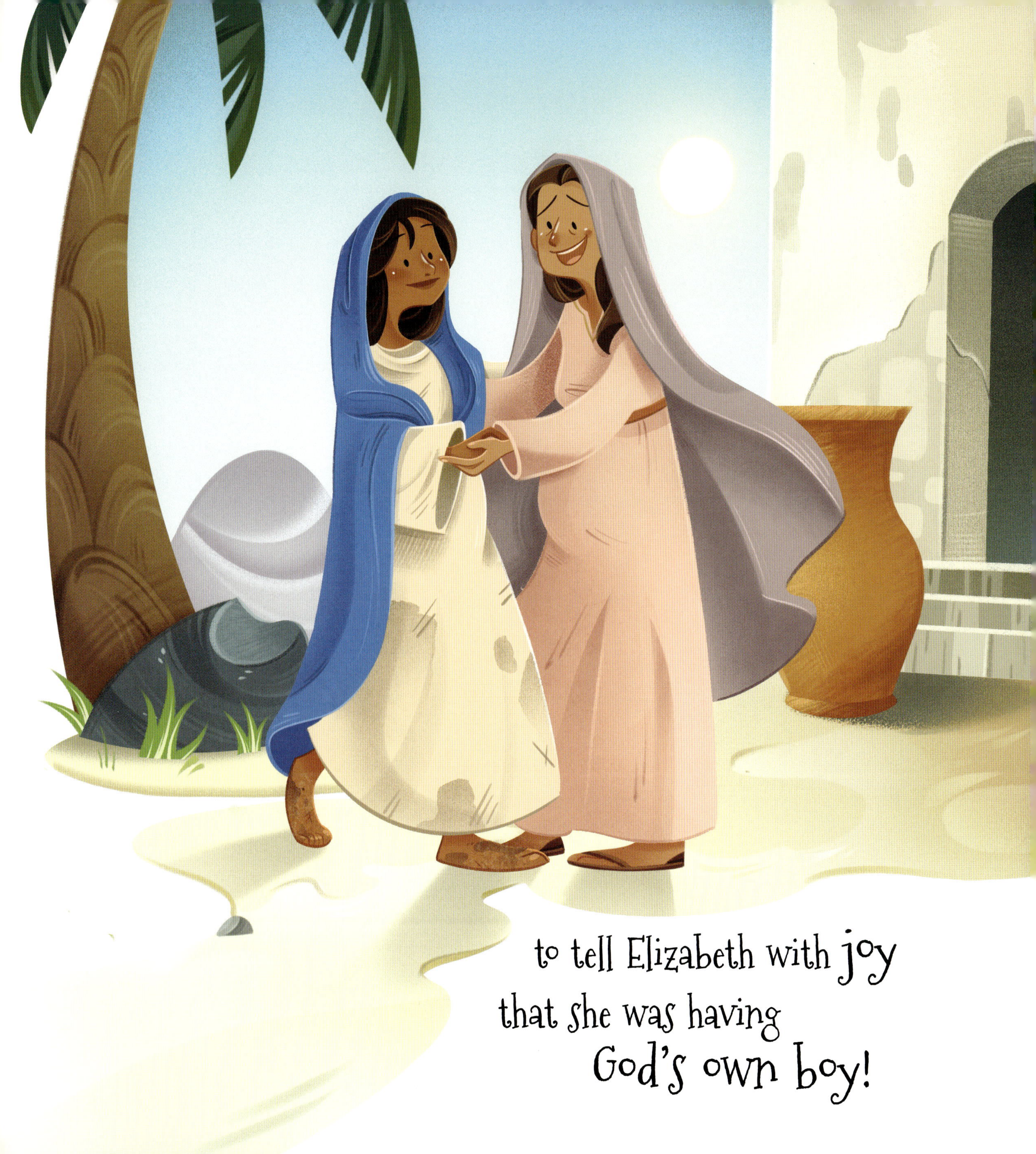

to tell Elizabeth with joy
that she was having
God's own boy!

First He was a child,
like you,

but over time He grew and grew.

Then on His feet, from place to place,
He shared God's love and spread God's grace.

Crowds walked or rode to hear Him speak—
the young, the old, the strong, the weak.

When Jesus healed the sick, they stood!
They jumped and danced
and said, "God's good!"

And all throughout His ministry,
Jesus helped the lost to see

that God rejoiced
when those astray
chose, instead,
to go God's way.

Then on His feet, so lovingly,
He took the cross to Calvary.
Then Jesus hung upon that tree
and paid sin's debt for you and me.

But, hallelujah,
Sunday morn,
as the women,
so forlorn,
tiptoed in to see their Lord,
their faith and joy were fast restored.

"He isn't here!" an angel said.
"He is alive—no longer dead!"
With joy renewed, on feet they ran
to tell the news of
God's great plan.

And ever since that Easter Day,
Christ's followers have found a way

with faithful feet from place to place
to spread God's love and share God's grace.

And how does God
describe those feet
that bring good news
to all they meet?
Does He call them funny? No!
Not at all! From heel to toe—

in sneakers, sandals, boots, or bare,
in a cast or in a chair—
He calls them LOVELY, big or small,
when they spread His love to all!

"How beautiful on the mountains
are the feet of those who bring good news . . ."
—Isaiah 52:7 (NIV)